KEY PEOPLE
OF THE CIVIL WAR

LORI MCMANUS

Heinemann Library
Chicago, Illinois

www.capstonepub.com
Visit our website to find out
more information about
Heinemann-Raintree books.

To order:
☎ Phone 800-747-4992
💻 Visit www.capstonepub.com
to browse our catalog and order online.

Edited by Megan Cotugno
Designed by Ryan Frieson
Illustrated by Mapping Specialists, Ltd.
Picture research by Tracy Cummins
Originated by Capstone Global Library Ltd.
Printed and bound in the United States of America
in Stevens Point, Wisconsin.
022013   007177R

15 14 13
10 9 8 7 6 5 4 3

Library of Congress Cataloging-in-Publication Data

McManus, Lori.
  Key people of the Civil War / Lori McManus. — 1st ed.
    p. cm. — (Why we fought, the Civil War)
  Includes bibliographical references and index.
  ISBN 978-1-4329-3913-7 (hc)—ISBN 978-1-4329-3919-9 (sc)
  1. United States—History—Civil War,
1861-1865—Biography—Juvenile literature. I. Title.
  E467.M434 2011
  973.7092'2—dc22
                    2009050040

Acknowledgments

The author and publishers are grateful to the following for
permission to reproduce copyright material:

Corbis pp. 19, 26, 39 (© Bettmann); Getty Images p. 15
(Hulton Archive); Library of Congress Prints and Photographs
Division pp. 6, 8, 9, 10, 11, 12, 13, 17, 18, 20, 22, 23, 25, 29, 31,
35, 37, 38, 40, 41; National Archives pp. 14, 16, 21, 33, 34, 36,
43; The Granger Collection, New York pp. 5, 7, 27, 42.

Cover photo of Abraham Lincoln reproduced with permission
from Library of Congress Prints and Photographs Division.
Cover photo of Jefferson Davis reproduced with permission
from Library of Congress Prints and Photographs Division.

We would like to thank Dr. James I. Robertson, Jr. for his
invaluable help in the preparation of this book.

Every effort has been made to contact copyright holders of
any material reproduced in this book. Any omissions will
be rectified in subsequent printings if notice is given to the
publisher.

All the Internet addresses (URLs) given in this book were valid
at the time of going to press. However, due to the dynamic
nature of the Internet, some addresses may have changed, or
sites may have changed or ceased to exist since publication.
While the author and Publishers regret any inconvenience this
may cause readers, no responsibility for any such changes can
be accepted by either the author or the Publishers.

Contents

Throughout this book, you will find green text boxes that contain facts and questions to help you interact with a primary source. Use these questions as a way to think more about where our historical information comes from.

Some words are shown in bold, **like this**. You can find out what they mean by looking in the glossary, on page 46.

Why Did We Fight the Civil War?

The American Civil War was fought over differences in lifestyles and ideas about the role of government. Divisions between the North and South began to appear soon after the **Revolutionary War** ended in 1783. By the late 1850s, these differences had grown very strong. In 1860, states in the South began to split off from the United States to create a separate government. The North entered into war with the South in order to keep the country together as one.

Differences in Lifestyles

During the early 1800s, people in the North and South developed different ways of working and living. In the South, farming **cash crops** was the main method of making money. Southerners depended on slaves to work hard in the fields and homes of their **plantations**. By owning slaves, Southerners could maintain a slow-paced and easy social life.

Eleven Southern states withdrew from the United States and created a new country called the Confederate States of America.

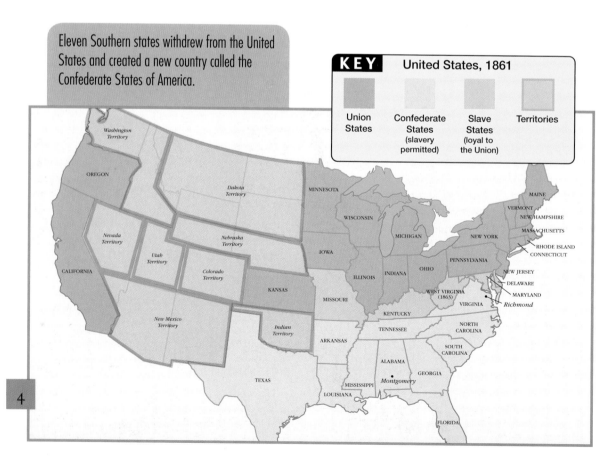

KEY United States, 1861

Union States | Confederate States (slavery permitted) | Slave States (loyal to the Union) | Territories

4

Northerners valued hard work on small farms. Factories and industry also began to thrive in the North. Many Northerners lived in cities rather than on farms. They worked in banks, factories, universities, and small businesses. By the 1830s, most Northern states had outlawed slavery. Most Northerners believed all people, including blacks, should be free to make their own decisions and be paid for their work.

Ideas About Government

People in the North and South also disagreed about the role of the national government. Southerners believed that each state's government should make the big decisions for its citizens, rather than the **federal** government. State governments in the South especially wanted to protect the right to own slaves.

In general, Northerners believed that the federal government should decide for all states whether certain practices were right or wrong. Northerners thought the federal government should prevent slavery from spreading to new territories in the west. Southerners strongly disagreed.

This is a photo of slaves on the plantation of James Hopkinson in 1862. The plantation was located on Edisto Island in South Carolina.

The Election of Lincoln

Abraham Lincoln was elected as president of the United States in 1860. Although Lincoln was personally opposed to slavery, he did not intend to outlaw it immediately. When Lincoln was sworn in as president, he stated, "I have no purpose, directly or indirectly, to interfere with the institution of slavery in the states where it exists."

Southerners did not believe Lincoln's words. In December 1860, South Carolina became the first state to secede, or break away, from the United States. By spring, 11 states had withdrawn from the **Union** and formed a separate nation, the **Confederate States of America**.

Lincoln tried to calm the country when he was sworn in as president. War erupted within five months.

BROTHER AGAINST BROTHER

Family members sometimes disagreed about which side to support during the Civil War. Disagreements were often strongest in families that lived in the states along the border between the North and the South. Some families were torn apart by their differences, with brothers actually fighting against each other during battle.

The War Begins

When the Confederate government was formed, Lincoln continued to hope that the country could be healed peacefully. Others believed that war was unavoidable. In April 1861, Confederate soldiers attacked federal troops and gained control of Fort Sumter in South Carolina. The Civil War had begun.

At first, the North fought primarily to keep the Union together. As time passed, the issue of slavery became equally important. The Civil War ended in 1865. The United States was preserved as one nation, and slavery was ended forever.

When Confederate troops fired on Fort Sumter in 1861, the Civil War began.

Who Wanted to Abolish Slavery?

In the 1830s, a growing number of Northerners thought that slavery should be stopped completely. These people were called **abolitionists** because they wanted to **abolish**, or do away with, slavery. By writing and speaking publicly about slavery, the abolitionists increased the tension between the North and the South.

William Lloyd Garrison

William Lloyd Garrison was a brave abolitionist in the years leading up to the Civil War. Born in 1805, Garrison grew up in the North. He learned the trade of publishing newspapers when he was a teenager.

William Lloyd Garrison published the anti-slavery newspaper called *The Liberator*.

> "On this subject [of slavery] I do not wish to think, or speak, or write, with moderation... I will not retreat a single inch, AND I WILL BE HEARD."
>
> —William Lloyd Garrison,
> *The Liberator, January 1, 1831*

The Liberator

In 1831, Garrison founded the nation's first anti-slavery newspaper called *The Liberator*. Garrison hoped to attract many readers, so *The Liberator* contained articles on subjects such as the military and the government. But his main focus was writing about the abolition of slavery.

Hated by Many

Garrison was soon hated by Southerners, who thought he was trying to start a rebellion among the slaves. He received angry letters and death threats. Even some Northerners thought Garrison was too extreme in his fight against slavery. Garrison wanted immediate **emancipation**, the freeing of all **slaves** at once, and equal rights for all.

Anti-slavery Societies

Garrison responded to criticism by increasing his efforts to end slavery. He helped start several important anti-slavery **societies**. These groups of people actively worked to free the slaves and improve the lives of free blacks. Garrison lived to see slavery abolished permanently during the Civil War.

Primary Source:
The Liberator, 1864

Garrison used *The Liberator* to fight for an end to slavery.

Thinking About the Source:

What, if any, words can you read in this newspaper?

Describe any other details that you can see in the image.

Frederick Douglass

Frederick Douglass was a well-known and important **abolitionist**. Born as a **slave** in 1817, Douglass secretly learned to read when he was young. He pursued learning whenever he had the chance. In 1838, Douglass escaped from slavery to freedom in the North.

Douglass soon became involved with the Massachusetts Anti-Slavery Society. He traveled around the North to speak against slavery. Douglass also wrote and published a best-selling autobiography. The book gave details of Douglass's life as a slave and discussed the damage slavery causes to individuals and society. Douglass's excellent communication skills and courage to speak out helped people in the North realize the need to end slavery forever.

Frederick Douglass became a famous anti-slavery spokesperson in the North.

"What, to the American slave, is your Fourth of July? I answer; a day that reveals to him, more than all other days in the year, the gross injustice and cruelty to which he is the constant victim. To him, your celebration is a sham."

—Frederick Douglass,
speech given July 4, 1852 in Rochester, New York

Sojourner Truth

Sojourner Truth never learned to read or write, yet she was a powerful voice in the abolition movement. Truth was born as a slave around 1797. She worked for a total of five masters. Truth gained her freedom in 1827, when New York passed a law that **abolished** slavery in that state.

While living with a Christian family, Truth developed a strong appreciation for religion, education, and public speaking. In 1843, she set off to preach about ending slavery. Truth held the attention of her audiences with her interesting personality and good sense of humor. Most importantly, Truth helped Northerners understand the harsh, cruel conditions of slavery.

Primary Source: Sojourner Truth

One of the ways that Sojourner Truth supported her work was selling calling cards. Her motto is written on the bottom. "I sell the shadow to support the substance."

Thinking About the Source:

Describe what you see in the photo.

Why do you think she chose this photo for one of her cards?

I Sell the Shadow to Support the Substance.

SOJOURNER TRUTH.

Harriet Tubman

Harriet Tubman risked her life to lead many slaves to freedom. Tubman was born as a slave on a Maryland **plantation** in 1820. She escaped to the North in 1849. Tubman worked hard, saved money, and went back the next year to help her sister and her sister's children escape.

Tubman returned to Maryland again and again over the next 11 years to help other slaves escape, including her parents and brothers. Tubman's dangerous missions earned her the respect of key **abolitionists**. They gave Tubman money for her work on the **Underground Railroad**, a secret network of people, hiding spots, and pathways that helped **slaves** escape to freedom in the North and Canada.

"I was the conductor of the Underground Railroad for eight years, and I can say what most conductors can't say; I never ran my train off the track and I never lost a passenger."

—Harriet Tubman,
as told to her biographer Sarah Bradford

During the Civil War, Harriet Tubman served as a nurse and spy for the Union troops.

Harriet Beecher Stowe

Born in 1811, Harriet Beecher Stowe used writing to express her views about the cruelty of slavery. In 1850, Stowe became very angry about the fugitive slave act, which demanded that Northern officials help return runaway slaves to the South. In response, Stowe wrote an anti-slavery novel called *Uncle Tom's Cabin*. Published in 1852, the book told a story from the perspective of several slaves and clearly showed the harsh conditions of slavery.

Over 300,000 copies of *Uncle Tom's Cabin* were sold the first year. The novel stirred up strong anti-slavery feelings in the North and anger in the South. It increased tensions that had been present for years, and that eventually erupted into the Civil War. According to Stowe's son, President Lincoln called Stowe the "little woman who started this great war."

Harriet Beecher Stowe's *Uncle Tom's Cabin* became a famous anti-slavery novel.

John Brown

John Brown believed he was meant to lead a **crusade** against slavery. Born in 1800, Brown became an **abolitionist** as a young man. Brown also became part of the **Underground Railroad**, helping slaves escape to freedom in the North.

Fighting to End Slavery

Unlike most abolitionists, Brown believed that fighting was necessary to end slavery. In 1855, Brown moved to the Kansas Territory, where people often argued about the issue of slavery. He became the leader of a small anti-slavery group. In revenge for a raid against the anti-slavery town of Lawrence, Kansas, Brown and his supporters killed five people in a pro-slavery town.

John Brown thought fighting was necessary to bring an end to slavery.

Harpers Ferry

After moving back to the East Coast, Brown began to prepare more seriously for a war against slavery. He needed money and weapons, and received some of each from a few Northerners. He needed more weapons for an army, however. On October 16, 1859, Brown and 18 men raided the United States **armory** in the town of Harpers Ferry, Virginia. They captured the armory for a while, but the attack eventually failed as U.S. marines fought against them. Brown was captured and convicted of murder and **treason**. He was put to death for his crimes in December 1859.

Tensions Grow

After his death, some Northerners began to speak positively about John Brown. They admired Brown's deep commitment to ending slavery. Southerners grew angry over this appreciation for a violent, anti-slavery man. Tension between the North and South increased sharply, leading to war within 18 months. Historians agree that John Brown's actions and punishment played a major role in starting the Civil War.

Primary Source:
John Brown's Execution, 1859

In this painting, Brown is being led to his execution in Charlestown, Virginia.

Thinking About the Source:

What is the first thing you notice in the image?

Is there anything you notice in the image that you can't explain?

Who do you think was the audience for this image?

Who Wanted the South to Secede?

As tension between the North and South increased, some people thought the South must completely break away, or **secede**, from the United States. These individuals, called **secessionists**, believed the differences between the North and South were too big to fix. They thought the South should form a completely new country.

Edmund Ruffin

Born in 1794, Edmund Ruffin was a strong supporter of secession. For most of his life, Ruffin was a farmer and food scientist in Virginia. In the 1850s, Ruffin began to publicly defend slavery and the need for secession. He saw these issues as the keys to protecting and improving the Southern way of life.

Ruffin joined the "Fire Eaters," a group of extreme proslavery **politicians** who urged the southern states to form a separate nation. Disappointed that Virginia was not the first state to secede from the **Union**, Ruffin went to South Carolina. He fired one of the first shots of the Civil War at Fort Sumter. Just before taking his own life in 1865, Ruffin wrote in his diary: "I here declare my unmitigated hatred to Yankee rule."

Edmund Ruffin was a die-hard Confederate.

Robert Barnwell Rhett was an early believer in secession.

Robert Barnwell Rhett

Robert Barnwell Rhett was the best-known secessionist in South Carolina in the 30 years leading up to the Civil War, publicly demanding that the South withdraw from the Union. Rhett was one of the leading "Fire Eaters" at the Nashville Convention of 1850. He left the convention disappointed that other Southerners did not yet agree that the entire South should secede. For his outspoken support of a separate Southern nation, he earned the name "Father of Secession."

...g the Civil War, the opposing governments were each managed by a dedicated ...der. President Abraham Lincoln sought to keep the United States together as one ...ation. Confederate President Jefferson Davis tried to organize an effective new government in the South. Both leaders demonstrated **patriotism** and a willingness to make sacrifices for the good of their citizens.

Abraham Lincoln

Abraham Lincoln is remembered as the president who saved the **Union** and freed the **slaves**. Born in 1809, Lincoln was raised on farms in Kentucky, Indiana, and Illinois as his family moved. He often read and studied on his own time. Lincoln eventually became a lawyer and a **politician**. He was known for his honesty and good judgment as a leader.

This portrait of Lincoln was taken in November 1863.

The Senate Race of 1858

In 1858, Lincoln was nominated for a spot in the **U.S. Senate**. When he accepted his nomination, Lincoln delivered a powerful speech about keeping the Union together. He declared, "A house divided against itself cannot stand. I believe this government cannot endure permanently half slave and half free. It will become all one thing, or all the other."

Lincoln then participated in a popular series of debates with his opponent, Stephen Douglas. Lincoln lost the election for the Senate, but people across the United States now recognized his name and understood his ideas about government.

Lincoln Becomes President

In November 1860, Lincoln was elected as the 16th president of the United States. Between his election and the time he actually took office in March 1861, seven states **seceded** from the Union. Lincoln believed that the **Constitution** made it illegal for states to secede. He wanted to bring the states back together peacefully, but he refused to bargain with the new Confederate government.

The Lincoln-Douglas debates of 1858 made Lincoln known across the nation.

The Fighting Begins

When the South attacked Fort Sumter in April 1861, Lincoln acted quickly. He increased the size of the military and purchased supplies for the troops. These decisions showed Lincoln's determination to save the **Union** even if it meant going to war. More states **seceded** and joined the Confederacy. The Civil War had begun.

Emancipation Proclamation

As time passed and the fighting continued, Lincoln decided that the Union could only be saved if the issue of slavery was resolved completely. With the **Emancipation Proclamation**, Lincoln freed all **slaves** in Confederate states that were still in rebellion as of January 1, 1863. Freeing the slaves was now an official goal of the Civil War.

The Emancipation Proclamation was issued by President Lincoln and granted freedom to slaves living in Confederate states.

Elected Again

Lincoln received criticism from some Northerners who thought he managed the war poorly. However, Lincoln easily won re-election as president in 1864. His victory demonstrated that people in the North had confidence in his ability to lead.

Lincoln was a tall man, as is clear in this photograph of him visiting Union troops in the field.

Lincoln's Death and Legacy

Shortly after the Civil War ended in 1865, Lincoln was killed by an actor named John Wilkes Booth, who was angry that the North had won. After Lincoln's death, Frederick Douglass summarized the president's legacy: "His great mission was to accomplish two things: first, to save his country from… ruin; and, second, to free his country from the great crime of slavery…. Dying as he did die… because of his fidelity to union and liberty, he is doubly dear to us, and his memory will be precious forever."

Jefferson Davis

Jefferson Davis served as the first and only president of the **Confederate States of America**. Davis graduated from the U.S. Military Academy at **West Point** in 1828. For the next seven years, he served in the U.S. Army.

Supporter of Slavery

Davis became a planter in Mississippi. Later, he served in the **U.S. Senate** and worked in the **federal** government as the Secretary of War. Davis publicly supported slavery and **states' rights**. When Mississippi seceded from the **Union**, Davis resigned from the Senate to join the Confederacy.

President of the Confederacy

Because of his military experience, Davis hoped to lead the Confederate armies. Instead, he was selected as president of the Confederate States of America. Davis initially hoped the South could be an independent country without any fighting. However, just a few months later, he approved the attack on Fort Sumter and entered into war with the North.

Jefferson Davis served as president of the Confederacy for four years.

Although he worked hard at his job, Davis made mistakes on some important decisions, like how to raise money to fight the war. People within his government criticized him for being stubborn. Others resigned because they thought he interfered too much in military decisions. Davis continued to direct his government, especially military activities, even though he was in poor health for most of the war.

After the War

Following the end of the war in 1865, Davis was held as a prisoner for two years. He was supposed to be put on trial for **treason**, but the case was dropped. Davis spent the rest of his life in Mississippi. Although he lost the war, Davis's hard work and willingness to suffer for the Confederacy earned him respect among Southerners.

Jefferson Davis is pictured here with other members of his government during the Civil War.

Who Were the Key Military Leaders in the North?

The North had the advantage of greater numbers of soldiers and weapons. However, early in the Civil War, the **Union** lacked military leaders with the kind of tough determination needed to win. Eventually, **generals** like Ulysses S. Grant and William Tecumseh Sherman led the North to victory.

Ulysses S. Grant

As a young man, Ulysses S. Grant attended the U.S. Military Academy at **West Point**. He graduated in 1843 and served in the army for 11 years. After resigning from the military, Grant tried several different jobs but was not successful at any of them.

Entering the Civil War

When the Civil War began, President Lincoln asked Americans to join the Union army. Grant agreed and was given the job of recruiting and training volunteers. He was promoted to a higher position within a few months. With the help of the navy, Grant's troops soon captured two Confederate forts and about 15,000 soldiers. President Lincoln heard about Grant's accomplishments and promoted him to major general.

Refusing Defeat

At the Battle of Shiloh, the Confederates surprised Grant's troops. Many Union soldiers were killed on the very first day, but Grant refused to back down. With tough determination, he reorganized his troops and launched an attack the next day. The Union troops won the battle.

In late 1862, Grant received orders to capture the Confederate city of Vicksburg, Mississippi. Grant was unsuccessful for several months. His military camp was captured, and his troops retreated. But Grant did not give up. He carried out a smart, unusual plan to surround the city. The Confederate troops at Vicksburg surrendered to Grant in July 1863.

Pictured here during the Civil War, Ulysses S. Grant was a master horseman and determined leader.

Commander of the Union army

Grant's determination and ability to win battles impressed President Lincoln. In March 1864, Grant became general-in-chief of all the armies of the United States. He immediately organized attacks on the Confederacy in different states at the same time. As part of the attacks, troops destroyed Southern railroads so the Confederates would be cut off from supplies.

Wearing Down the Confederacy

In May 1864, Grant led **Union** troops into a two-day fight at the Battle of the Wilderness. Many soldiers on both sides were injured and killed. Instead of retreating, Grant ordered his troops to pursue the Confederates. He was determined to wear down the Southern soldiers with constant fighting. A few days later, Grant wrote, "[I] propose to fight it out along this line if it takes all summer."

"If you see the President, tell him from me that whatever happens there will be no turning back."

—Ulysses S. Grant,
spoken to journalist Henry Wing in 1864, at the Battle of the Wilderness

President Lincoln is shown here with Grant (to his left). When pressured to replace Grant, Lincoln was claimed to have said, "I can't spare this man. He fights."

Grant (left) allowed Lee (right) and the Confederate officers to keep their belongings, horses, and weapons when they surrendered at the Appomattox Court House.

Ending the War

By September of 1864, Grant's plan to capture key Confederate cities around the South was working. In April 1865, Grant's pressure on the Confederate army forced it to leave its capital city of Richmond, Virginia. Soon after, Grant's troops cornered the Confederate army at Appomattox Court House. Grant gave Confederate General Robert E. Lee the chance to surrender. He offered Lee conditions that would help the Southern army maintain some pride after their defeat. Lee surrendered to Grant, and the Civil War ended.

William Tecumseh Sherman

As a young man, William Tecumseh Sherman attended the U.S. Military Academy at **West Point.** After graduating in 1840, Sherman served in the army for 13 years. He later became an effective and popular leader of a military college in Louisiana. When Louisiana **seceded** from the **Union** in 1861, Sherman resigned and returned to the North.

> "You people of the South don't know what you are doing. This country will be drenched in blood… War is a terrible thing! You mistake, too, the people of the North. They are not going to let this country be destroyed without a mighty effort to save it…"
>
> —William Tecumseh Sherman,
> *as stated to Professor David Boyd in 1860*

Fighting for the Union

In May 1861, Sherman joined the Union army. Soon Sherman was assigned to serve under General Ulysses S. Grant. At the Battle of Shiloh, Sherman showed great bravery under pressure when his forces were caught by surprise. For the next two years, Sherman's troops experienced both wins and losses. Despite this mixed record, Grant had confidence in Sherman's leadership skills.

Sherman's "March to the Sea"

When Grant became general-in-chief, he chose Sherman to lead all Union armies fighting along the Mississippi River. Sherman invaded Georgia and captured the Confederate city of Atlanta. He then planned a long march across the state to Savannah, Georgia. In the cities and along the way, Sherman's troops destroyed military buildings, businesses, and railroads to cut off Confederate communications and supplies. Sherman captured the city of Savannah on December 21, 1864. His determination and success helped to end the Civil War in April 1865.

> "I beg to present you, as a Christmas gift, the city of Savannah."
>
> —William Tecumseh Sherman,
> *in a telegram to President Lincoln, December 1864*

Primary Source:
William Tecumseh Sherman

This portrait of General Sherman was done in 1865.

Thinking About the Source:

What do you notice first about this portrait?

Is there anything missing from this portrait?

If someone made this today, what would be different? What would be the same?

Who Were the Key Military Leaders in the South?

Two of the best-known Confederate **generals**, Robert E. Lee and Thomas "Stonewall" Jackson, served in the United States armed forces before the Civil War. Dedicated, skillful generals like Lee and Jackson gave the Confederates an advantage, even though they had fewer supplies and soldiers than the North.

Robert E. Lee

Many historians consider Robert E. Lee the greatest general of the Civil War. Lee was born in Virginia in 1807 and later attended the United States Military Academy at **West Point**. He graduated at the top of his class. Lee spent the next several years planning and building forts, harbors, and waterways with the U.S. Army **Corps of Engineers**. During his 32 years in the U.S. armed forces, Lee also served in battle zones and as the head of the academy at West Point.

Strong Ties to the South

In early 1861, President Lincoln asked Lee to lead the **Union** army against the Southern states that had **seceded**. Although Lee agreed with the Union's beliefs, he chose to serve his home state of Virginia instead. When Virginia seceded in April 1861, Lee resigned from the U.S. military and became commander of the armed forces in Virginia.

> "With all my devotion to the Union and the feeling of loyalty and duty of an American citizen, I have not been able to make up my mind to raise my hand against my relatives, my children, my home. I have therefore resigned my commission in the Army…"
>
> —Robert E. Lee,
> *written in a letter to his sister, April 20, 1861*

Robert E. Lee led the Confederate troops because of loyalty to his home state of Virginia.

Commander of the Army of Northern Virginia

In 1862, Confederate President Davis put Lee in charge of the powerful Army of Northern Virginia. The **Union** army had already invaded Virginia, but Lee stopped it from capturing the Confederate capital of Richmond. Lee left forces to guard Richmond while he moved north to confront a new Union army advancing through the center of Virginia.

Unsuccessful in the North

Lee invaded the North two different times. He advanced into Maryland in September 1862. Union soldiers there found a copy of Lee's battle plans and knew he had split up his army. Lee lost many soldiers at the Battle of Antietam and retreated back to Virginia. In 1863, Lee moved north into Pennsylvania, only to suffer a major defeat at the Battle of Gettysburg.

Stuck in Petersburg

Lee returned to Virginia to protect the capital city of Richmond. However, large numbers of Union troops forced Lee's army to stay in Petersburg for 10 months without new supplies or help from other Confederate armies. Many of Lee's soldiers left the army during this time because of sickness and disappointment. Lee finally withdrew from Petersburg on April 2, 1865. Seven days later, he **surrendered** to **General** Grant. Other Confederate generals followed Lee's decision, and the Civil War ended within a few weeks.

Dignified in Defeat

Soon after the war ended, Lee asked for an official **pardon** and for his U.S. citizenship to be restored. Though his citizenship was not restored during his lifetime, Lee devoted the rest of his life to setting an example of dignified behavior for ex-Confederates.

> "After four years of arduous service marked by unsurpassed courage and fortitude, the Army of Northern Virginia has been compelled to yield to overwhelming numbers and resources."
>
> —Robert E. Lee,
> *in his Farewell Address to his army, April 10, 1865*

Robert E. Lee is considered to be one of the most talented generals in American history.

Thinking About the Source:

When do you think this photograph was taken?

Why do you think Lee chose to pose without his uniform on?

33

Thomas "Stonewall" Jackson

Thomas "Stonewall" Jackson was a dedicated and disciplined commander in the Confederate army. As a young man, Jackson attended the U.S. Military Academy at **West Point**. Jackson then served in the U.S. Army during the **Mexican-American War**, receiving several promotions for his good judgment and disciplined behavior. Later, Jackson taught at the Virginia Military Institute.

Jackson's Nickname

When the Civil War began, Jackson began to train new soldiers for the Confederate army. He soon took command of the Confederate troops at Harpers Ferry, Virginia. Jackson earned his nickname at the First Battle of Bull Run. His troops fought with courage and steadiness against the advancing Union soldiers. Another Confederate **general** rallied his own troops by shouting, "There stands Jackson like a stone wall."

Thomas "Stonewall" Jackson led his troops into battle with skill and courage.

"We must make this campaign an exceedingly active one. Only thus can a weaker country cope with a stronger; it must make up in activity what it lacks in strength."

—Stonewall Jackson, *written in a letter, 1863*

Winning Characteristics

Jackson was promoted to lead greater numbers of troops in the Army of Northern Virginia. He became Lee's most valued general. Jackson possessed winning qualities: boldness, wise use of the Virginia landscape, skill in planning, and the ability to inspire his troops. He excelled in the Battles of Antietam, Fredericksburg, and Chancellorsville. By 1863, Jackson commanded more than half of the Confederate army.

Unfortunate Death

During the Battle of Chancellorsville, Jackson was accidentally shot by his own troops. Jackson survived the shooting, but died of pneumonia eight days later. When Jackson died, the Confederacy suffered the loss of a skillful and inspiring leader.

> "I see from the number of physicians that you think my condition dangerous, but I thank God, if it is His will, that I am ready to go."
>
> —General Jackson,
> *on his deathbed in May 1863*

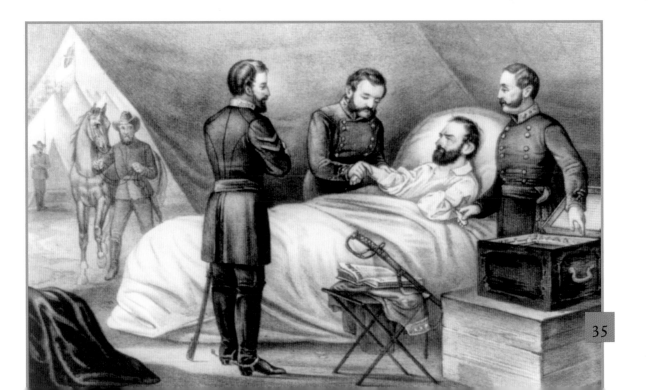

Which Women Participated in the War?

In the 1800s, women rarely worked outside their homes. However, during the Civil War, some courageous women decided to help on the battlefields. They worked in military camps as cooks, nurses, messengers, and even spies.

Clara Barton

For her work as a nurse during the Civil War, Clara Barton became known as "The Angel of the Battlefield." Born in 1821, Barton was an intelligent child. As an adult, Barton became a skilled and respected teacher. Later, she was hired as the first female clerk in the U.S. Patent Office in Washington, DC.

Bringing Supplies to the Troops

When the Civil War began, Barton organized the collection of blankets, food, clothes, and medical supplies for the **Union** troops. She also carried the supplies to the battle zone. Barton followed the sounds of gunfire so she would be among the first to arrive where need was greatest. She immediately prepared food for the troops and distributed bandages and medicines.

Clara Barton served as a nurse on the battlefields of the Civil War.

Working as a Nurse

Barton soon began nursing on the battlefield. She assisted with surgeries, bandaged wounds, and comforted dying men. She was often covered with gunpowder and blood. Although she witnessed violent scenes, she saw the Union army as her responsibility. Barton willingly cared for wounded soldiers throughout the entire war.

Founding the Red Cross

After the war, Barton organized efforts to find out what happened to missing soldiers. In 1881, she founded the American Red Cross. This organization still exists today and provides practical help in emergencies, natural disasters, and wars.

I was strong ~ and I thought I ought to go to the rescue of the men who fell -:

But I struggled long and hard with my sense of propriety~ with the appalling fact - that I was only a woman. whispering in one ear - and the groans of suffering men. dying like dogs.. unfed and unsheltered. for the life of the very Institutions which had protected and educated me- thundering in the other-.

I said that I struggled with my sense of propriety ~ and I say it with humiliation and shame -. Before God and Before you I am ashamed that I thought of such a thing -

But when our armies fought a Cedar Mountain I Broke the shackles and went to the field

**Primary Source:
Clara Barton's Lecture, 1866**

"I was strong and I thought I ought to go to the rescue of the men that fell."
—Clara Barton

Thinking About the Source:

What other words, if any, can you read in the document?

What can you learn from examining this document?

Does it change any opinions that you had about women's role in the Civil War?

Mary Edwards Walker

Mary Edwards Walker was the only female surgeon to serve on the battlefields during the Civil War. At the start of the war, Walker volunteered to work for the Union army. Because she was a woman, Walker was only allowed to be a nurse and assistant surgeon at first.

In 1862, Walker worked as a field surgeon near the **Union** front lines. She received food and a tent for her service. Later, the army offered to pay her for her work as a surgeon. In 1865, Walker was awarded the Congressional Medal of Honor for her courageous efforts on the battlefield. Walker remains the only woman to have ever received this high award.

Mary Edwards Walker was the only female surgeon to serve on the battlefields during the Civil War.

Rose O'Neal Greenhow worked as a spy for the Confederacy. This photo of Greenhow and her daughter was taken in 1862.

Rose O'Neal Greenhow

Rose O'Neal Greenhow served the Confederacy as a spy during the Civil War. Born in 1817, she earned the nickname "Wild Rose" early in life. Greenhow grew into an intelligent, outgoing woman who became friends with government and military leaders in Washington, DC.

When the Civil War broke out, Greenhow sided with the Confederacy. She used her social connections to spy on the Union army. The secret information she passed along helped the South to win the First Battle of Bull Run. Greenhow was put in prison for spying. However, she continued to get important messages to the Confederate troops.

After two terms in prison, Greenhow traveled to Europe as a messenger for the Confederacy. On the return trip, her boat capsized and Greenhow drowned. She was buried with full military honors, an unusual reward for a woman.

Which Artists Captured Images of the War?

Poets, writers, and photographers used words and pictures to explain Civil War experiences. Through art, they also expressed the feelings of people affected by the war. Because of these artists, Americans have a permanent record of what the war looked and felt like.

Walt Whitman

Walt Whitman, an American poet and journalist, captured the confusion and pain of the Civil War years in his writing. During his early adulthood, Whitman worked as a printer and a teacher. Later, he started a weekly newspaper and worked as an editor and writer.

Soon after the Civil War started, Whitman published his poem "Beat! Beat! Drums!" as a patriotic message about joining the Union army. In 1862, Whitman traveled to Washington, D.C. and onto the surrounding battlefields to look for his injured brother. Whitman was deeply affected by the sight of wounded and suffering soldiers. He volunteered as a nurse in the military hospitals for the rest of the war.

Walt Whitman wrote about his experiences working in hospitals during the Civil War.

Whitman wrote about his experiences in the hospitals in an essay titled "The Great Army of the Sick." In 1865, Whitman published his war poems in a book called *Drum Taps*. These poems expressed the sights, sounds, and feelings of the Civil War.

"AN ARMY CORPS ON THE MARCH"

With its cloud of skirmishers in advance,

With now the sound of a single shot snapping like a whip, and now an irregular volley,

The swarming ranks press on and on, the dense brigades press on,

Glittering dimly, toiling under the sun—the dust-cover'd men,

In columns rise and fall to the undulations of the ground,

With artillery interspers'd—the wheels rumble, the horses sweat,

As the army corps advances.

—Walt Whitman,
published in Drum Taps, 1865

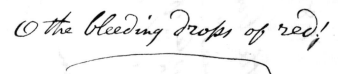

O the bleeding drops of red!

O CAPTAIN! MY CAPTAIN!

BY WALT WHITMAN.

I.

O CAPTAIN! my captain! our fearful trip is done,
The ship has weathered every track, the prize we sought is won,
The port is near, the bells I hear, the people all exulting,
While follow eyes the steady keel, the vessel grim and daring.
But O heart! heart! heart!
~~Leave you not the little spot~~
Where on the deck my captain lies,
Fallen cold and dead.

II.

O captain! my captain! rise up and hear the bells,
Rise up! for you the flag is flung, for you the bugle trills:
For you bouquets and ribboned wreaths, for you the shores a-crowd-
ing:
For you they call, the swaying mass, their eager faces turning.
O captain! dear father!
This arm ~~I push beneath you.~~ *beneath your head*
It is some dream that on the deck
You've fallen cold and dead.

III.

My captain does not answer, his lips are pale and still:
My father does not feel my arm, he has no pulse nor will.
~~But the ship,~~ The ship is anchored safe, its voyage closed and done: *and*
From fearful trip the victor ship comes in with object won! *sound.*
Exult, O shores! and ring, O bells!
But I, with silent tread,
Walk the spot my captain lies
Fallen cold and dead.

**Primary Source:
"O Captain! My Captain!"**

One of Whitman's most famous poems, "O Captain! My Captain!" was written to express his grief over President Lincoln's death soon after the North won the Civil War.

Thinking About the Source:

What words, if any, can you read in the document?

Whitman revised this poem several times. This document was his 1888 revision.

Does this change how you view the source?

Mathew Brady

Mathew Brady documented the Civil War in photographs. Brady owned his own photography studio in New York. He also opened a studio in Washington, DC, so he could photograph the nation's leaders. In the 1850s, Brady was known as one of America's greatest photographers.

> "From the first, I regarded myself as under obligation to my country to preserve the faces of its historic men and mothers."
>
> —Mathew Brady
> *as told to an interviewer in 1891*

Mathew Brady took hundreds of photographs during the Civil War.

Brady's photographs allow us to better understand the Civil War.

Recording History

When the Civil War began, Brady decided to record the battles and experiences of soldiers in photographs. Brady organized a group of over 20 photographers to help him accomplish this task. He also bought battlefield photos from private photographers so that his collection would be as complete as possible.

The Reality of War

During the First Battle of Bull Run, Brady got so close to the fighting that he was almost captured by the Confederates. In 1862, Brady displayed photographs from the Battle of Antietam in his New York studio. He shocked the public by actually showing dead soldiers in the photos. For many Americans, this was the first time they had ever seen real images of battlefields. The *New York Times* reported that Brady had brought "home to us the terrible reality and earnestness of war."

Brady did not earn much money from his Civil War photographs. Yet his remarkable collection gives us a glimpse of what life on the battlefield was like. He was one of the first people in the world to use photography as a way of recording history.

Timeline

1831	William Lloyd Garrison begins to publish *The Liberator*
1840s	Abolitionists like Frederick Douglass and Sojourner Truth travel around the North to speak about the issue of slavery
1850s	Harriet Tubman helps hundreds of slaves escape to freedom on the Underground Railroad
1852	Harriet Beecher Stowe publishes *Uncle Tom's Cabin*
1859	John Brown is convicted of treason for his raid on Harpers Ferry and put to death for his crime
November 1860	Abraham Lincoln is elected as the 16th president of the United States
February 1861	Jefferson Davis becomes president of the Confederate States of America
April 1861	Southerners, including Edmund Ruffin, fire on Fort Sumter; the Civil War begins
June 1862	General Lee becomes commander of the Army of Northern Virginia
January 1863	President Lincoln's Emancipation Proclamation takes effect
May 1863	General Stonewall Jackson dies

March 1864	General Grant takes command of the Union army
December 1864	General Sherman completes his March to the Sea, capturing the city of Savannah, Georgia
April 1865	General Lee surrenders to Grant at Appomattox Court House; the Civil War ends
November 1865	Mary Walker Edwards recieves the Congressional Medal of Honor
1865	Walt Whitman publishes *Drum Taps*
1881	Clara Barton founds the Red Cross

Glossary

abolish do away with; put an end to

abolitionist during the Civil War period, a person who wanted to end slavery in the United States

armory storage place for weapons

cash crop crop such as tobacco, rice, or cotton that is grown in large amounts to be sold for cash

Confederate States of America group of 11 Southern states that seceded from the United States in 1860-1861

Constitution fundamental law of the United States that went into effect in 1789

Corps of Engineers branch of the U.S. Army responsible for military and some public building projects

crusade determined attempt to bring change based on the idea that it is the morally right thing to do

emancipation state of being free from bondage

Emancipation Proclamation document issued by President Lincoln that granted freedom to slaves living in Confederate states when those states did not return to the Union by January 1, 1863

federal related to a central or national government, as opposed to the governments of individual states

general military officer holding a high position of authority

Mexican-American War conflict between the United States and Mexico from 1846 to 1848

pardon forgiveness that is given by the president for a crime

patriotism great love of country

plantation large farm or estate that is worked by a large number of laborers, like slaves

politician person who holds a government position

Revolutionary War war against the British for American independence, fought 1775–1783

secede break away from something

secessionist prior to the Civil War, a person in favor of Southern states withdrawing from the United States

slave person who is the property of another

society organized group of people linked together for a religious, political, or scientific purpose

states' rights rights and powers the states possess in relation to the federal government, as guaranteed by the Constitution

surrender quit a battle, admitting defeat

treason crime of acting to bring down or defeat the government

Underground Railroad network of secret routes used to help slaves escape the South to gain freedom

Union United States of America

U.S. Senate upper body of lawmakers of the U.S. government, which has fewer members who serve longer terms than members of the House of Representatives

West Point United States military academy located at West Point, New York; many Civil War generals, North and South, attended West Point

Find Out More

Books

Abnett, Dan. *Abraham Lincoln and the Civil War*. New York: PowerKids Press, 2007.

Armstrong, Jennifer. *Photo by Brady: A Picture of the Civil War*. New York: Atheneum Books for Young Readers, 2005.

Ford, Carin T. *Daring Women of the Civil War*. Berkeley Heights, NJ: Enslow Publishers, 2004.

Gillis, Jennifer Blizin. *The Confederate Soldier*. Mankato, MN: Compass Point Books, 2007.

Robertson, James. Robert E. Lee: *Virginia Soldier, American Citizen*. New York: Atheneum Books for Young Readers, 2005.

Silvey, Anita. *I'll Pass for Your Comrade: Women Soldiers in the Civil War*. New York: Clarion Books, 2008.

Websites

http://americancivilwar.com/kids_zone/index.html
The Kids Zone shares the music, flags, letters, cooking, pictures, and people of the American Civil War. This website also provides titles of good books and DVDs on the Civil War.

http://www.socialstudiesforkids.com/subjects/civilwar.htm
Do you want to learn more about the Civil War? The Social Studies for Kids website includes interesting information about the causes, battles, and people who were involved.

DVDs

The Unknown Civil War Series: Gettysburg (DVD). Mpi Home Video, 2009.

The History Channel Presents The Civil War (DVD) (1999). History Channel DVDs, 2007.

Index